A Willow in Bloom

Jasmin Lowe-Velazquez

BookLeaf Publishing

India | USA | UK

Presentation by *BookLeaf Publishing*

Web: www.bookleafpub.com

E-mail: info@bookleafpub.com

ISBN: 9789360948894

First edition 2024

I'd like to dedicate this to my family, my friends (Jeremy, Skyler, and Emma), and to the Eastside Native American Education Program, which gave me my Native name. I love you all!

Dissociation

I wake up, my head already hurts
But I'm just tired

I try to eat breakfast, I can't
My stomach is killing me
But I'm just tired

Class is too loud, I can't pay attention
No matter how hard I try
But I'm just tired

I feel like I'm not even there, I'm in my head
Watching a movie I can't process
But I'm just tired

Heart rate high, energy low
I slept for 9 hours
But I'm just too tired

I'm shaking, I'm nauseous
This happens everyday, no reason to fuss
I'll be ok, I'm just tired

Anxiety

My heart feels heavy
Why is everyone laughing?
Nothing's even there

Water

When it rains
All is calm
The sounds of nature
Everything is one
Rain, nature, earth

Shopping

I've always felt weird
Buying myself things
Whether it's a need or a want
Or something I want that I know I'll use
I always hesitate

People think I have a shopping addiction
I really don't
I want many things
But I've always felt weird buying them
Whether it's a need or a want

Shoes

I've never been much of a shoe person
But my parents are

I've always worn a black pair of sneakers
But they never made me feel like a star

If I feel cute
I'll wear black boots
But they're heavy, so I can't get far

If I'm in the house, I'm in my slides
The black platforms I wear inside

So many shoes
Yet I pick the same three

Sneakers, boots, and slides
Sneakers, boots, and slides

Pollution

There's so many pollutants in the world
Gas, smog, trash

But at the root of it all, is people
Greed, corruption, incompetence

Not only do we pollute the world, but other
people too
Abuse, toxicity, gaslighting

I love the way we love
Eachother, nature, the world

But I hate the way we hurt
Eachother, nature, the world

Nausea

I have this thing
Where I'm always nauseous
So obviously, I'm cautious
Of what I eat, of what I drink
But I never throw up

It gets even worse
Whenever I'm sad
I'm already sick, from whatever I had
But now I won't eat, I can't when I'm hurt

I never eat when I'm sad, I don't know why
I could be starving, but I can't even try

It gets worse when I'm nauseous
Because I'm already cautious
Of what I eat, of what I drink
But I never throw up
So it's all stuck inside
The sadness, the sickness
Feeling like you can't survive

Overstimulation

I wish that I could go out more
To concerts or family events
But the noise in my ears leaves my body sore

I can feel my clothes on my skin
I'm irritated by everything
I'm angry and I can't keep my feelings in

It's not my fault that everything's loud
I didn't chose these issues
I wish I could tolerate crowds

Cupcakes

One day, a cupcake appeared on the counter
She was beautiful, with cookie dough for
frosting
I will always remember our encounter

I asked mother if I could have a bite, she said no
I stared for hours, waiting for my chance
There was a reason for the wait, as mother had
already had her go

She tried it, said it might be a dog treat, but why
the chocolate then?
Was it fake? Was it real? Could I have it?

In the end, I ate it. 10 out of 10.

Dirt

Dry
In winter, with
Rain, it's mud
Tasty dirt

Earth

This world is a beautiful place
The way the trees sway
How the birds sing

I wish we treated the Earth the way it treats us
Giving it food, care, and shelter
But we don't

We owe everything to our planet
Our lives and our homes
But we never act like it

Memory

I can't remember
My childhood is a blur
When did this happen?

Doctors

There's so many types of doctors
I wonder which one I need
A cardiologist to fix my heartache?
Or a neurologist to fix my brain?
Maybe a psychiatrist to tell me what's in my
head?
Or a pulmonologist to help me breathe?

Potato

Peace
Order
Time
All
Truth
Over it?

Grocery Stores

Going grocery shopping is such an experience
Getting ready for something so simple, so
mundane

Walking around in circles for hours
Trying to remember what you need and what
you don't

Figuring out what you want to eat for the next
week or two
Spending $300 on four people's food, for most
of it to go bad

We should just order pizza

Soup

Sachet for stock
Onions and beef
Unified in one, big
Pot

Autism

Autism can be many things

You could try too hard to socialize, practicing
scripts for different situations
Or you could go nonverbal, and not socialize at
all

People may think you're a genius, others may
think you're stupid
Sometimes you're both, sometimes you're
neither

You may have many friends, finding comfort
with your people
Or you may get bullied, and have no one at all

Maybe you love loud music, but only in your
headphones
Maybe you can't survive festivals or concerts

Sounds like two different people
They're both me

Christmas

It's Christmas today
I wish I could still experience the wonder of
Christmas as a child
Decorating the tree
Making cookies
Opening presents
Obviously I can still do these things
But as I get older, holidays just get sad
In fact, everything gets sad
Yeah I love gifts and I adore a chocolate chip
cookie
But where's the wonder? Where's the love?
Where's the fun?
Can I have some?

Homework

I've never understood homework
Or the concept of "busy work" at that
We get nothing from this but extra practice
Practice for things we won't use
If we're not getting much credit, or any credit at
all, why do we do it?
And why can't we use our notebooks on tests?
Why can't you have us experiment with different
careers to find what we love?
Or teach us how to pay taxes?
Wash dishes?
Buy a house?
All of this homework that we'll never be able to
use when building a life in our own home
How useless.

Masks

Masks
As in pandemic?
As in autism?
As in hiding who you are?
I think they're all for protection in some way Or
for trying to fit in
Protect yourself from a disease
Protect yourself from others seeing who you are
You gotta do it
You gotta be like everyone else
No you don't
You can be you
You can show everyone who you are
But if it's a masquerade party, please be on
theme

Reflection

I've finished my writing
I never thought I'd do something like this
It's been a long time since I've written something
of my own volition
Since I've written something of my own feelings
In third grade I hit a bad literature rut
I rarely wrote or read
I'm in 11th grade now
I've been "recovering" since 9th grade
Hopefully this starts something new,
Or reignites something old